GR HOWL

AND OTHER POEMS

An Anthology
by the Pets
of the Great Poets

Edited by

DAVID SHEVIN

GR

HOWL

AND OTHER POEMS

CARPENTER PRESS

Columbus, Ohio

Published by:

CARPENTER PRESS
P.O. Box 14387
Columbus, Ohio 43214

Copyright © 1990 by David Shevin

Second edition

Cataloging-in-Publication Data

Shevin, David, 1951-
   Growl & other poems : an anthology by the pets of the great poets
/ edited by David Shevin.
     p.   cm.
   ISBN 0-914140-15-9 : $6.95
   1. Pets--Poetry. 2. Pets--Poetry. 3. Parodies. I. Title.
   II. Title: Growl and other poems.
   PS3569.H47G76 1989
   811'.54--dc20   89-22189
                   CIP

ACKNOWLEDGEMENTS

Many thanks to the editors who first printed and promoted these yips, meows, growls and whinneys: *Apalachee Quarterly, Beatniks From Space #6, Pig Iron: Humor, Plains Poetry Journal, Slipshod Review, Sometime the Cow Kick Your Head,* (Bits Press), Upstairs at Arnold's and *Zoo Poems* (Pudding Press).

CONTENTS

CONTENTS

CONTENTS

CONTENTS

INTRODUCTION

When the Institute for Animal Humanities reissued such classic works of Alternate Species Literature as Meow Tolstoy's *War and Fleas*, and Tabby Orwell's *Homage to Catatonia*, the inquiries for possible projects began to arrive in deluges. While response to every good idea from the field is far beyond the reach of our limited staff, we hope in this volume to help satisfy the requests of countless housepets and their owners who commented on the coincidence of literary style, content, and attitude among animal writers and the people they lived with. While the similarity of pets and owners is a commonplace, and while the canon of English language poetry is deeply treasured, this volume represents the first collection of poems by the pets of the great poets.

That the writing represented here begins with Modern English poets is the result of practical obstacles, rather than editorial dictum. It is a fact of cultural history that literacy became prominent among humans well before other Western species. Examples we have of Early and Middle English animal lyrics are of greater interest to the dogged scholar than the general reader. They are unrefined and in most cases, barely comprehensible.

As serious research in Animal Literature is a relatively new science, we faced the inevitability of past neglect. Preservation and transcription of manuscript has been laborious. Our Institute's documentation reveals that the training papers of some species were more accessible to our workers than others; it demands notice here that housecats have most notably kept their writing in a more protected, cleaner state of preservation than any other species. As writers, however, they have not been as prolific as have dogs.

While we have tried to be as comprehensive as creaturely possible in assembling this compilation, the reader will find some obvious omissions. We are still unable to locate authenticated manuscripts of either "The Wife of Bat's Tail" or "Tabsalom and Akittyphel." None of the once-famous works of Bounce (Alexander Pope's watchdog and companion) is available as far as we presently know. Highwind, a dog belonging to Philip Larkin, has dismissed his puppy training poems published under the title *The Whitsun Wettings* as embarrassing juvenilia, and refused us permission to reprint.

These and many other obstacles were present in the preparation of this anthology, certainly. Despite them, the feeling at the I.A.H. is that the present volume is our proudest project to date. We are delighted to present the work of the more familiar poets to a wider audience, and to make available so many all-too-neglected wildlife writers for the first time. A special thanks is owed to Kitty Lights Books, who granted us permission to reprint from the controversial "Growl." Also thanks to Hopper & Crow for "Lassie" and THE SLIPSHOD REVIEW for "Thirteen Ways of Looking at a Herring."

In describing the poets themselves, we have used the popular rather than scientific classifications of genus for identification to the general readership. When a more particular species or family has been made evident by the poet, it is used.

For encouragement and perseverance, the Institute owes its deepest gratitude to the patient candidates for graduate degrees in Creative Writing and Literature, the part-timers and adjuncts, mimeo-stained editor/publishers, teachers and students who have tilled these fields for love again and again. Without their work and example, this project could not have begun.

David Shevin, Chaircreature
Institute for Animal Humanities
Cincinnati, Ohio
December, 1984

PREFACE

archie debates the stuff of literature

well boss i wonder what makes
the stuff of literature
a bookworm i know says he likes all of the classics
because the paper in those fancy editions are high in rag fiber
and help keep down his cholesterol or else the pages are old
and brittle and almost digested already
he was halfway through the tragedies of shakespeare at the time
and he was angry at hamlet the melancholy dane
this isn't even about dogs at all says my friend
and look how this supposedly thoughtful and introspective prince
addresses the other species

what is a man
if the chief good and market of his time
be but to sleep and feed question mark   a beast no more

i ve seen feeding and sleeping men
in libraries and universities who do not bear
the dignified title of beast he continued
furthermore if hamlet was not eating something disagreeable
before slumber and if he did not sleep perchance to dream
then how would he have known the truth about claudius and gertrude

says i the prince did not downgrade sleeping and eating
but he glorified imagination and action and besides
hamlet also said this of the animals in case you haven t eaten that far

let hercules himself do what he may
the cat will mew and dog will have his day

this brings me roundabout to the book on your desk
called growl and other poems
which carries a dedication to me
for my own vers libre bardic efforts
and includes poems by many visionary animals
while the book underrepresents insects
my friend and i still devoured it in fact
he gave it a rave review and said it was delicious
so sweet and so cold

archie

for archie the cockroach
il miglior fabbro

THE PASSIONATE LEOPARD TO HIS LOVE

by That Girl (Christopher Marlowe's cat)

Come live with me and be my cub,
And we will up on stout trees rub
In Ethiop's warm streams and wadis
We'll sun our long and tawny bodies.

And we in brightness' range will meld
With forest objects 'cross the veldt,
And by the Niger where the hawk
Sings madrigals in squick and squawk.

And I will make for thee a nest
Inside the antelope's warm breast,
A cafe where we'll feast a term
In belly of a pachyderm;

And nest thee in a wooly cover
Which from our shepherds we did tear;
Deep and lovely, earthy tones
Garlanded with shepherd bones.

And I'll give thee a tribesman's shield,
Sweet gazelle from yonder field;
And if these offers thee won't snub,
Come live with me and be my cub.

The forest toms will beat and boom
For thee and me as we far roam:
Safe with me from the hunter's club,
Now live with me and be my cub.

A VALEDICTION: FORBIDDING WHINING

by Dorset (John Donne's hound)

As swift greyhound pups run wildly away
  And hide behind trees, and play with the ball,
While their owners file off with John to pray
  Breathing their holy words and all;

So let us run, kick up our paws
  No whimp'ring like a penned-in mutt;
'Twere travesty of canine laws
  To whine like juice in sickly gut.

Bones hidden in earth bring discovery.
  Dogs have long reckoned what objects meant;
The trepidation of the trees,
  The fresh surprise of rabbit scent.

Stupid earthbound schnauzer love
  Where lost in scent will not admit
Of parting, for that smell will prove
  The animal that sweated it.

But we by supreme love canine
  Know dogs' secret lovebound trails:
The mystery of doggie hind,
  Reckless floppy ears and tails.

Our supper bowls therefore are one
  Although I run, you run with me.
No separations, as the gun
  And hunter make twin ecstacy.

If they be two, then we are two
  As stiffened pointer twins are two
As Narcissus and the pond are, too.
  One's a dog-face, so are you.

4

We circle wide and then draw near
Still we're free to chase and roam.
It takes a lot of twinness here
To make a dog house a dog home.

How delicate your whisper'd pant;
We rollick when the day is done.
I chase my tail in circles and
I come to end where I've begun.

SONG: TO CILIA

by Sidney Pennshurst (Ben Jonson's guppy)

Drink to me only with thine gills
And thou wilt never drown:
We'll scamper wildly 'round the bowl
Where watery pleasure's shown.
Hear how the godly bullfrog trills,
Now bubbles rise hose-blown.
As Ben the tank with breadcrumb fills
I'd have thee for mine own.

A plankton nosegay I sent thee
Seaweed-tied, in shell of snail.
'Twas for thy honor; do not depart,
In shyness turn they tail.
Thou to the gravel's end did flee
Hid in the plastic whale.
Return to me, my seaweed heart
Grows soggy ere I fail.

from SONNETS #18

by Ophelia (William Shakespeare's horse)

Shall I compare thee with a summer's dray?
Thou art more steady, and just as calm of mind.
Thy shanks may wobble as the boards may sway,
Good help these days is very hard to find:
Oftimes Apollo's star makes thee to slow
And creak like wagons creak with heavy load,
Yet trimmed by summer's heat a patient glow
Makes thy complexion gold as purchase owed.
The cart may crash and fall to tiny splinters
By chance reduced to spoil in damp and dew.
But time refines thy lines, thy gaits and canters;
My thoughts are rich with love and poor with glue.
As long as horses do hard work apply,
This length be not as long as my heart's joy.

TO ALPACA, FROM THE POUND

by Lucasta (Richard Lovelace's sheepdog)

When love with unconfined woofs
Comes romping through the yard,
And my dearest Alpaca hoofs
It toward me, breathing hard;
My sweetest dog with funky name--
In her warm fur I lie
And chuckle. How the larks above
Know no such levity!

When dinner time comes rolling round
With no Kibbles and Bits,
We'll hunt our scraps close to the ground
Surviving by our wits.
We may weep on tearstreams to dawn
But light makes sorrow flee,
The bats who boink the belfries blind
Know no such levity.

When like obedience trainers, I
Imperatives command
The glory and the majesty
That angels understand;
Confinement seems no more so dark,
My Little Chickadee;
Alpaca, with our yip and bark,
We yowl such levity.

Stone walls do not a hydrant make
Nor iron cage a bush;
And quiet mind can't tension break
When you've an itchy tush.
Still I have freedom in my being
In trunk of every tree
I've nourished--may my wishes bring
Them joy and levity!

ON THE LATE MASS OF CURS IN PIEDMONT

by Samson (John Milton's mastiff)

Avenge, O Lord, thy slaughtered Saint Bernards
Lying scatter'd on the Alpo mountains cold
Whose bones are stolen and whose withers fold
Lifeless on their crests. In thy deck their cards
Were dealt from bottom: when our foredogs still roamed
In Babylon and worshipped with the chow-chows
They kept the herds preserved, both sheep and cows.
Now slain by bloody Pinscherese who foam
At mouth, who for lunch scarfed their pups.
Forget not: for they go where doggies go
Although their echoed howl still interrupts
The peace of mountains, thou may'st perceive the low
Growl of a martyr, as in clouds he sups
On Angel's slipper, o'er the Puritan's toe.

TO HIS COY MATTRESS

by Sackeyes (Andrew Marvell's opossum)

Had we the time to sleep, and rest
This coyness, Sealy, were no jest.
I'd lie on Morpheus' breast so large
And let the Sominex take charge.
Ten winks and forty, shallow breath
I'd sleep through earthquakes, floods and death.
Ten years I'd dream of field and farm,
Ten more to turn off the alarm.
I envy the guiltless sleep of Pontius
Who betrayed the Lord, then fell unconscious!
The yogin can sleep upon his knees;
On their heads they drowse in the Antipodes;
The sloth sleeps sound slung from his toes;
A flea dreams of blood in the oxen's nose.
Yet when I come to thee for rest
I am your strange, unwanted guest.
The bed's a place for warmth and peace
But none like me can there cop Z's.
Yes I, my bed you do rebuke
Till the conversion of the nuke.
No rest will come, I turn and twist.
I should have been a somnambulist
For he asleep who can move and rise
At least can get his exercise.
How dearly we wish for what we lack
But none so as the insomniac!
I'd sleep now if I could, I feel.
I'd sleep at work, behind the wheel,
At play, at church, while on my bike,
I'd sleep through couplets I don't like.
I'd best Sysiphus by taking
To the top of the mount this stone of waking
To push it o'er the crest to spill
Into the very bowels of hell.

THE SANITY OF ALL WOODLY THINGS

by Berryman (Anne Bradstreet's weasel)

In the wood, sanity, so sane say I
Oh! Sanity, sane all under the sky;
As pulpits preach madness, storms still long rage
And folks put my brethren in lock and in cage,
What beast or his progeny can still now claim
"Lo, I have found peace in a world that is sane?"
The fox for a time lopes the forest with ease,
In sanity's folds he's at home and in peace.
Then, soon enough, he's beset on by dogs
Or snared in the steel trap's mechanical jaws.
What worth is his beauty when hooked by that snare?
How silly the senses when raging for air!
What blossoming vixen won't contemplate sorrow
Knowing she too may be snared on the morrow.
There's a way through the crazy woods not known by hawks
Or the vicious bobcat or the quickening fox
Where the sane lull of sunlight caresses a glade
And horses roam slow in the change and the shade.
Such stock are such stoics, when madness about
Comes into their ears with a shriek and a shout--
They flick with their ears the dumb horseflies of rage
And dream simple dreams about cactus and sage.
A rat thinks of minks as a bear knows of snows
As the dog knows the way by the scents in his nose
So let the mind go free, though sceptics may scowl
And horse-like, imagine a sane world in order
Where horses know naught of a trap or a border.
Consider, like horses, a slow pace of thought,
Digestion, and heartbeat, and what you have sought
Will beautify, grow, and like leaves from the tree
Of life, you will richness and crown'd fullness be.
The simmer of sanity's summer is found
In forests of fairness, in grass on the ground,
In clearings of clarity, circles of sound,
And girding the mountains, by cool rivers bound.
When nature decrees that you come here to stay
Then all that's insane will ne'er stand in your way.

11

from **JUBILATE AGNEW**

by Jeoffry (Christopher Smart's cat)

For I will consider my man Spiro.
For he is the servant of the Living Wad, duly and daily serving
Him.
For at the first glance of sense and right, he is off to the East
to aviod it in his way.
For this is done by wreathing his tongue seven times round with
elephant grace.
For then he steps aside to dodge the flak, which the press visits
upon his oath.
For he revels in pranks to work it in.
For he issues his words and considers only himself.
For he has a hard time distinguishing himself from a potatoe.
For this he comprehends in ten degrees.
For first he has skin so thin it is almost transparent.
For secondly his most prominent feature is lumps.
For thirdly he expects to fry or bake.
For fourthly he looks up for his instructions.
For fifthly he has eyes that perceive only dirt.
For sixthly he grows fat and tubular, that he may not be
interrupted by his neighbors.
For seventhly his roots are shallow.
For eighthly he revels in shallowness.
For ninthly the nutritionists spurn him.
For tenthly, on the Farm Exchange, potatoes are currently going
for seven cents a bushel.
For having considered the Wad and himself he will consider his
constituents.
For if he meets another potatoe, he will dance in gladness.
For when he confronts an effete intellectual snob, he will
crush it with impugnity.
For when he finds a Fat Jap, he will ridicule it.
For when his day's work is done, his work on *The Canfield
Decision* begins.
For he counteracts the Evil Soviet Empire with this dashing,
irresistable Vice President of the United States.
For his hero seduces the glamorous Secretary of Health,
Education and Welfare.

For he shrinks from the sun and walks by night.
For he is of the tribe of the Vampire.
For he is an instrument for children to learn fear upon.
For the Spiro Cat is a term of Social Disease.
For he is a mixture of obscenity and ignorance.
For he plods steadily with iggy things between his toes.
For he learns grace under pressure.
For he knows the taxman as his mad brother.
For he knows Frank Sinatra will bail him out to the tune of
    a million.
For he can tread to the measures of "My Way."
For he is of the Lord's flukes, and so calls mercy to himself
    perpetually--"Poor Spiro! Poor Spiro! The *Post* has bit my
    throat!"
For he has made a great impression in Hell for his signal
    services.
For he is a major stockholder in the Coors brewery.
For the divine spirit enters him and he knows that he is a
    potatoe.
For he is docile and can thrive in the dark.
For he can converse with the skunk cabbage and the fungus.
For he can sit in the drainer and the roaches will shun him.
For he is wedded to rot.
For confronted with his own vulgarity, he responds, "I yam what
    I yam."
For his motions are the most profound of any tuber.
For he's a creep.

AURIOLES OF INNOCENCE

by Beulah (William Blake's cockatiel)

To see the World in a Grain of Seed
And a Birdbath in drizzly March Weather
Hear Eternity's Winds in the rustling Weeds
And Infinity in a Feather.

A Rhode Island Red in a Pen
Doth perturb the Divine Hen.
A henhouse fill'd with Australauks
Smells of Rot on Satan's Socks.
A Ruffed Grouse 'neath the hunter's Sight
Fills Blood-thirsties with delight.
Autumn sees the Mallards go
Honking of Michelangelo.
The Curlew with his funny Bill
Stabs the Fascist's ugly will.
The Penguin waddles, fish in tow
Across God's grainy, seemly Snow
& as the Penguin's stately dres't
Just so's the Atheist depres't.
The Peregrine, who's tagged on leg
Doth cause the Capitalist to beg.
A Gyrfalcon high on his perch
Is in himself the bird's own Church;
Or, soaring past the burning Sun
Maketh palsied soldiers run.
The Ptarmigan, his feathered Foot,
The Chimney Swallow's wing of Soot
Are worth more in their Joy and Hope
Than a Cardinal to the Pope.
Angel Dodos descend to watch
The webb'd & handsome Booby hatch.
The brute who makes the Child to cry
A Hornbill pokes him in the Eye.
A miser clips the lovely Rose
& Paradise Birds fly up his nose.
A fox disturbs the Chicken Coop
& boils in Hell in Bird's Nest Soup.

The Banker & the cruel Cop
Upon them lofty Pigeons drop.
A Budgie in a Worker's flat
When happy makes them gay & fat,
But if that Budgie wants for Food
A Vulture hunts the couple's Blood.
Nothing makes the Cultured yawn
Like pink Flamingoes on the lawn.
The Puffin can escape the Zoo
The Auk or Toucan do it, too
& free, the Forester can see
Them fly away above the Tree.
The falconer doth in Pain delight,
He might as well go fly a Kite.
The Landlord evicts with poison'd Pen
But Someday he must pay the Wren.
He who the neutron bomb doth place
Shall soon have Egg upon his Face.
The Egret nesting on the Mount
Reflecteth Life's Eternal Fount.
Every morn and every eve
Birdbrains are born who don't Believe
birdbrains are born who don't Believe
& Shrikes are born just to Deceive.
Ugly lies to us do Sing
When we see not through the Wing--
Lies we have in our Hearts to best
In souls well-nurtured in the Nest.
Fowl appear in Earthbound Form
To those who Grovel for the Worm
But doth a Flighty Form display
To those who Fly in Realms of Day.

A DEAD, DEAD DOZE

by Bonie Doog (Robert Burns' terrier)

O my love's in a dead, dead doze
  That's freshly snored i' the shaw;
O my love she meets my body
  A-comin' through the raw.

My daemon beastie, thou art fair,
  The fairest i' the wurld;
I will love thee til the knots
  In all the trees are squrl'd.

Till elephants forget, my dear
  And pigs fly a' the day;
O I will still get wet, my dear
  While mice gang aft a'gley.

So fare thee weel, my dearest doog
  And fare thee weel for now!
For I am bound away, dear one
  To a doog show in Glasgow.

THE SOLITARY REEFER

by Annette (William Wordsworth's falcon)

Behold her sitting in the field,
Yon Squirrel-toothed, ozoned Highland lass!
Rockin' and rollin' by herself
And smokin' up the grass!
Alone she dries and cleans the buds
As to her song the woodchuck thuds;
O listen! Vales of leaf and petal
Reverberate to heavy metal.

No ghetto-blaster e'er did boom
More strident sound to street-dance troops
Who tumble 'mid the fast rap rune
In high, white polished boots:
So sweet a solo, duet or trio
Was ne'er heard on a home stereo
Interrupting night's soft ditty
Among the discos of the city.

No one steps forth to Name That Tune--
Is this an improv rings the valley
Echoing nights of Fifties moon
With Berry, Fats, and Buddy Holly?
Or some new hit across the glade,
A tune our market's not yet played?
I watch her at the vesper's turning.
A solitary reefer in her hand burning.

Whate'er she sang with wild panache
It thundered like Rock and Roll Heaven;
I saw her packing up her stash
And now she's climbing the stairway to Devon.
I listened from a branch gone bare
Then winged away to higher air;--
Her song I carried past the cloud
Where Hendrix turns his amp up loud.

KUBLA KHAT
Or A Vision in a Catnap, A Fragment

by Porlock (Samuel Taylor Coleridge's cat)

In Kokomo did Kubla Khat
Run chasing insects merrily:
While Al, the wretched river rat
Contented in the pantry sat
  'Mid sugar, oats and tea.
So twice five pounds of sifted flour
Were scattered widely on the floor;
And there were puddles of diet Shasta
With half-nibbled Twinkies dropped into the lot
And here brown rice and whole-wheat pasta
From a macrobiotic kick now long forgot.

Meow! that porch where kitties romp 'neath boards
Smoothed down by rain and stained with grog!
A shaded place! As cluttered and curious
As where Stubb the Cat in identity crisis
Went barking, thinking he was a dog!
And from this cave, like tiny mice a'scamp'ring
Came bursting marvels for a kitty's pampring.
A bursting udder hugely from there grew:
In whose sharp spurts of milk there spew
Chunks of beef and egg and fish aquiver
By feline wailing for her devilled liver:
And 'mid this milkbath in hazy gloamin'
Kubla Khat felt rich and Roman.
The milk ran around the house, if you please,
Then dripped on below with a rat-a-tat-tat
Where it came to a place oft forbidden to cat,
The cellar where they hang the cheese!
But a portent made Kubla feel weak in the knees--
His mother's voice prophesying fleas!
  The puddles of the milky stream
  Faded in with the drops last seeping
  Where dreamy visions rise like steam
  And left a relic for cat's keeping.

18

It was Paradise within an inch,
A flea collar that didn't pinch!

A damsel with a batting bell
In this dream I plainly saw
It was a pretty Siamese
Batting music to the trees
Singing of Catalonia.
And if I heard again
That rough, staccato chant
I know it would fire my brain
I could reconstruct that fount--
I'd drag that cheese from underground--
The dinner dish! The eggs and fish!
And who approach, even if a hound
Would never dare disturb my wish
My glowing eyes! My killer claws!
Yes, scribe your fate with trembling paws
Let whiskers curl to catly chorus,
For I've defied all catly laws
And I've shared dinner now with Morris.

SO WE'LL GO NO MORE WITH ROVER

by Prometheus (George Gordon, Lord Byron's dog)

1.

So we'll go no more with Rover
  Across the neighbor's lawn,
To knock the trash cans over,
  Since he's shut inside 'till dawn.

2.

We won't feed on last night's quiche
  While he's locked up for the night,
For the dog's worn out the leash
  And must curb his appetite.

3.

Though the pail's without its cover
  And the trash is on the street,
Yet we'll go no more with Rover
  To get a bite to eat.

JANUARY

by Shepherd (John Clare's cat)

The icles gnarl the gutter pipe
At window & the gutter snipe
Is froz to metal, frails his wings
Dying all God's glory sings
The sternel eaten by the kitty
Never dreamed a grub so pretty
The fotherer & milkmaid joll
The wind thru cyrstal stoney knoll
Drabbled all despite the cold
So even Preacher Creature smild
How closen in the winter morn
The nimble hare is brightly born
Sturts in the goodly cottage door
Where kitties shit & dumb dogs snor
Karl Manx would jumble up & down
Among the workers of the town
Where sutted dark satanic mills
Display sad lives as hunters kills
& Karl would cry as wearies go
& caw we need a minstrel show
The actor cats sung from their housies
Love to eat dem little mousies
Dog poet wore a look of pain
Cirging on but he would fain
Love one wi eyes of soft spring rain
& fermentation in her brain
He clammed from the mizzled race
Wot never loved a kitties face
The happy copper down the street
Makes the time to beat his meat
Then booger-nozed a stingo drinks
At pub what luck he never thinks
Martins teem the vaunted sky
But coppers know not where nor why
Nor how nor taste nor sight nor sound
Nor their ass from a hole in the ground
The actor cats will singing sweet

21

Mousies what I love to eat
Singing tails and ruzz like balls
Of darkness thru the vestry walls
An extasy the wintry lunch
To hear a mousy bone go crunch
Or hear a story we adore
Dave dropped the eggs on kitchen floor
Or when the cat the scalpel siezed
& stole the vetrenaryun's ovaries
Oer fallows snowflakes gently stir
Life's sweetest poems are writ in fur

STANZAS
Written in Distemper, near Naples

by Caleb W. (Percy Bysshe Shelley's spaniel)

1
The sun is warm, the clouds form bones,
　The butterflies dance in gold light,
Blue waters' motion at shore hones
　A blade of sand in tan and white.
The dog in hare scent would delight
On more ambitious afternoons
　But Springtime's regimen takes flight
And Summer's pleasure softly moans
Soft peace and deepest sleep for lousebit ones.

2
The scrub and brush on distant hill
　Shows paths where wild dogs run and leap.
The sound of lapping waves and trill
　Of birds calm creatures proud to sleep.
　I heel at shore and try to keep
My mind in tune with rabbit kill.
　The natural world's off counting sheep.
I growl my song alone until
How quick! The gangley wrens fly in close drill.

3
Arf! Arf! I have nor cold nor worms
　Nor warming fire nor calm around,
But memories of Spezia's fold
　Of ocean where poor Shelley drown'd.
　I listen for sweet Bysshe's sound:
"His Master's Voice," as charged in art.
　I listen, though just waves abound.
Within me, puppy tears just start
To climb toward Doggie Heavens of the Heart.

4

I blink to sea two times, and thrice.
  My brain grows agitated, wild--
I fall upon the thorns of lice!
  I bleed! My country life's defil'd!
  The hour when simple angels smil'd
On me and Shelley have now fled
  As dreams flee from a waking child
On schooldays as he crawls from bed
And morning's challenge pounds his addled head.

5

In stasis, some lament I smell.
  Do I look like I tuppence care?
Scents mean so little, truth to tell
  As my lost heart returns aware
  To presence. Scoffers have nowhere
For tears--Although they moan and gripe,
  I'll walk unloved down Roman shore,
Between the seaweed, sludge and tripe
Where seagull breeze my mawkish tears will wipe.

LA BELLE CHATTE SANS MERCI

by Flea Hunt (John Keats' cat)

You got a hairball, puss-in-boots,
　Is that what makes thee cough?
You got a lesion in your ear,
　Your whiskers falling off?

The canary's long flown from his cage,
　Is this your meditation?
The neighbors' dog left with them
　On a two-week vacation.

Is that a scratch above thy eye
　Or hast though caught a chill?
I know how hard it is to take
　The antibiotic pill.

"I met a kitty in the weeds
　A longhaired Persian, coat of white.
Her claws were sharp, her teeth were long
　She shone like winter's night.

"I made a collar for her neck
　And rhinestone baubles for her brow.
She saw me as her lover cat
　And made sweet meow.

"I led her down a bushy path
　Where we jumped quick as foxes,
And as she rolled she sweetly sang
　Of perfumed litter boxes.

"She brought me catnip, dandelions,
　And field mice, sassy fat
As catgut sings her purr still rings:
　'I love thee, cat.'

"I was in kitty heaven when
   She curled into a ball
So I destroyed the furniture and clawed
   The papered wall.

"She wept until I groomed her shank
   And there I dreamed of skeins of yarn
But then the saddest dream passed since ever
   I was born.

"I saw bobcats and panthers too
   Pale ocelots, their tails they dragged.
They catcalled, 'La belle chatte sans merci
   Hath thee in bag!'

"I saw their fangs in moony gloom
   As bare as talons on a hawk
So here on damp and mucky knoll
   I rude awoke.

"And thus my melancholy air
   Weariness and agitation
Though the neighbor clan's got Bowser on
   A two-week vacation."

ANNABEL LEECH

by Rovermore (Edgar Allen Poe's wolfhound)

It was many and many a year ago
  In a condo by the beach
That a puppy I puppy loved whom you may know
  Was attacked by Annabel Leech,
And this puppy she lived with no other thought
Than to share with me each to each.

She was a pup and *I* was a chit
  In this condo by the beach,
And we yipped with yip much more than a bit
  'Till there came dreaded Annabel Leech--
'Twas a love that the Hounds of Heaven know
  But can never mortals teach.

So ethereal! skyward! and long ago
  In this condo by the beach
The agent of Satan slimed into our bliss
  In the form of Annabel Leech
So that her litter came crowding 'round
  In bloodsong beyond my heart's reach
And bore her toward Puppy Pastures
  From this condo by the beach.

Bird dogs with holy terriers
  With envy would rant and preach:--
Yes! that the puppose (as all dogs know,
  In this condo by the beach)
That the worm came out of the sea, soaking
  And croaking, cruel Annabel Leech!

But what we had outshone the love
  Of those better groomed than we
  Of many more pedigreed
And neither the muttheads in Heaven above
  Nor the fleabags who hang by the beach
Can ever make waver the rage that I feel
  Toward nefarious Annabel Leech:--

For the dogs never howl but I wrench in my bowels
  At the scurrilous Annabel Leech;
And the gnats never bite but I gasp at the sight
  Of my memory of Annabel Leech;
And as tides roll in sure, I lie down demure
And I think of my darling, my bride and my cur
  Chosen daughter of the beach
  As I'm a lost son of a beach.

CROSSING THE BEAR

by Higglety Piggletey (Alfred, Lord Tennyson's koala)

Beehive in the branch there
  And plainly it's for me!
And may there be no groaning of the bear,
  When I climb up the tree.

A hive so rich and teeming never sleeps,
  Preoccupied beyond repose,
So any bear may have implanted there
  A stinger in his nose.

The plan is this: by starlight
  I'll take them unawares
And may there be just honey sweet
  For happy bears;

For while the tree climbs not to Paradise
  So far from hurt and care
I'll pray I haven't paid too high a price
  Once I have fed the bear.

OUT OF THE KENNEL, ENDLESSLY BARKING

by Paumanok (Walt Whitman's dingo)

Out of the kennel, endlessly barking,
Out of the Doberman's maw, the woof of the angel,
Out of the full moon's matings
Beyond the racetrack and doghouse where the puppy crawled from
  the rags, solitary, soft.

Down from the jostling goslings,
Up from the darkness of the city pound where lost lapping dogsouls
  crowd cages,
Up from the marsh pond, the duck egg miasma
Electric, gleaming life embrace,
Up the sleep of cicadas, seventeen years underground,
Out from the clovered briar patch and enigma,
Whupping the young poet upside the head,
From Peabody's Improbable History,
And the pages of the *Voyage of the Beagle*,
Out of sweet labor's elemental mist,
Over under around and through,
From the panting of fast run through cranberry thicket,
From malamutes shaking in Arctic far winds,
A dog, in saliva throwing his head to the sky
And by this token a pup again
I, grunter of thorns and trash,
Borne of the madness of houndstooth and harechase,
Rolling on the carpet, terrorizing drapes,
Making a bed in the basement,
A recollection recollect.

A morn in the yard
When New Jersey dumpsite was downwind and radishes sprouted,
Two fleabag felines imported from Persia
Crouched watching a cardinal chit in her nest
And I'd seethe, contemplate my chain,
As the caterwauling commenced.

Light of heaven, over here!
On windowsills, rugs and the table
On grassy spot, where I bask!

We together!
Like the Cat Gods of the Egyptians
Like Krazy Kat and Ignatz
Knew the Sun unbounded
Warm us home!
Nap! Nap! Nap! Nap!
In warmth and sacred fatness!

I was astonished.
They didn't seem to sense me.
Cats are so dumb. That matins mist
When the she-cat pawed the tabby with infinite incomprehension--
It was like an apparition of unpleasantness.
Or a vision to be chased.

Thenceforward into an eternity of thickets and garbage,
Over the roaring of city fences
Out to tempt Spuds MacKenzie at his frat party
In the academic halls of Disco Tech,
And I hard the cathowl continue.

Meow! Meow! Meow!
Where we're going! Where we've been!
Why we're here! Where's dinner? Blow off fleas,
Winds of the ocean! What is to be done
With the mouse
Once the head's eaten?

High are the clouds like a night on catnip,
and some insecticides can get you off as well.

Purr! Purr! Purr!
I call to you, fat cat, from the legions of litters
Which came to this shore on the catwalks of schooners,
Certainly you know the coming of heat, the spray of frenzy
You must know who I am, my love.

I am he who sniffs with infinite amour!

The party had gone on for long enough.
I, Paumanok, aching, sweating, stupefied, hater of cats, mask of
  the dog's mission,
Growled a single growl
And saw the streak of Persians cross the far yards.

Yeeeeeeeeow! Yeeeeeeeeeeow!
O piercing throat! O mighty cry!
O luckless be when death's chords fanfare the waning moon!
O the dog mimics not the call of the sun
but the son of a bitch is nearby!

Thither my love!
I am sick and sorrowful.
I'm getting my ass out of here.

The yowls diminished,
Yet the world continued, trash cans in the street clattered,
The mail carrier again tried to invade my territory,
Yet nothing remained of the cats
But their scent in the dust they raised. I felt good. I sang my
  own rich songs for hours.
The sea was beckoning, and I was up for a run.
Every dog has his day, they say, except the one whose tail got
  stepped on.
He's got a weak end.

OH, SWAGMAN! MY SWAGMAN!

by Paumanok (Walt Whitman's dingo)

Oh swagman! My swagman! The hobo's journey's oer,
The wallaby is in the stew with clams so it won't sour,
Down yonder by the billabong the kiwi scratches dust,
At your side sniffs the platypus, his eyes dulled weak
  with trust.
  But a dingo's heart grows heavy
   In Australia's matin mist;
    In outback's brush my swagman lies
    Fallen down dead pissed.

Oh swagman! My swagman! Get up to greet the sun!
For you the rabbits jump the hedge--for you the wombats run!
For you the healthy kangaroo--his lengthy leap he launches,
For you the fatted jumbucks all roll over on their paunches.
  Here swagman! Dear hobo!
   Your doggie's every wish
    Is that you'd pay attention, but
    You're drunker than a fish.

My swagman moans and curses, his lips are caked with crud.
Some snagger steals his tucker bag half-hidden in the mud.
The billy's toppled in the coals, its contents burnt and ruined,
But off somewhere the sheep shearer still sings a lusty tune.
  Swagman, when stupor passes
   And your dead eyes start to see
    Then won't you come waltzing
    Matilda with me.

DROVER BEACH

by Seadog (Matthew Arnold's shepherd)

The road is still tonight,
The truckstop's calm, and moonshine's
On the shirt; --the trucker's out like a light,
Snores and is gone; the bleating sheep reminds
Me of our cargo bound for farms down coast.
Come to the truck, sweet with dieselley brine!
As cold carbon wafts betwixt pole and post
Where the salt air whisks scrubbing with night tide's wind
Hear! You will hear the engine clunk
And rest while sheep kick high, and graze,
When free from grates, up the scrub hill
Happy as a pin in the head of a punk--
Without thought as the wet, rolled sand softens in waves,
The sense of loss in plankton's gunk.

Benji long ago
Heard it on the laugh track, and there raced
In his mind the silly stop and go
Of a dog's life; you
Know by now the travelling noise of haste
But by this concrete night, we sniff and study slow.

For the Bone of Gnawledge
Was once, too, stopped at an all-night diner,
Kicked like the crumple of discarded Arby's sacks.
But tonight I listen
To the oily waves where fish-skins glisten
Holding my panting breath
In the silv'ry first fingers of morning star's shiner
And trembling fever of a puppy stung by ticks.

Good dog! Let us be warm
To each other! for the moment, which appears
To fly before us, devoid of all earthly fears
As calm as a painting of MacDonald's farm
Hath no reality, nor food, nor goal in sight,
Nor substance, nor rest, nor break of its pace;

And here we are as on a parkling space
Kept confused by alarms and sirens and searchlights bright
Where big Dunlop semis crash by night.

"'Hope' is the thing with whiskers"

by Higginson (Emily Dickinson's hamster)

"Hope" is the thing with whiskers--
And pouches in its cheeks--
that runs within the running wheels--
And almost silent--squeaks--

And lovely--in the pantry sat--
So busy with the oats--
Who can combat the nasty Cat--
And rip its stupid throat--

I've seen it in its little cage--
So tiny yet so brave--
I had with me a BLT.
It asked a leaf--I gave.

BONZO

by Just So (Rudyard Kipling's gibbon)

I headed for the Troubador to sip a pint o'stout.
The bouncer said, "Look on the wall! 'No Animals!' Get out!"
Gorillas sittin' at the bar made googley eyes at me.
Once outside, I said to meself, I told this chimpanzee:
O it's Bonzo this an' Bonzo that an' "Bon, don't give me
grief."
But it's "Thank you, Mr. Reagan" when they play
"Hail to the Chief."
They play "Hail to the Chief," my monks, they play
"Hail to the Chief."
It's "Thank you Mr. President," and sing "Hail to the Chief."

I went to the Oval Office, as bright as bright could be;
They welcomed crim'nal maniacs, but none so bright as me.
They had their Secret Service thugs pitch me beyond the gate
But when it came to movies--Lord--they had me on the set!
For it's Bonzo this an' Bonzo that an' "Bonzo, wipe yer snot!"
But "Banana juice for Bonzo!" when the comp'ny's on the lot.
The comp'ny's on the lot, my monks, the comp'ny's on the lot.
O "Banana juice for Bonzo" when the comp'ny's on the lot.

You can jibe at evolution though a chimp once paid yer rent
An' cut off poor schoolchildren though they 'aven't got a cent
An' in their schools teach "Seven days the Lord made all the
earth
Where life just at conception starts, and neatly ends at birth."
Then it's Bonzo this an' Bonzo that an' "Bonzo, shut yer gob."
But it's "look at that cute monkey" when the Late Show's on the tube.
The Late Show's on the tube, my monks, the Late Show's on the tube.
It's "Which one's Ron, which Bonzo?" when the Late Show's on
the tube.

We aren't "cute monkeys." No sir! And not subhuman, too.
We're thoughtful, sentient beings more compassionate than you.
So if we show you up, Ron, and you want to shoot an' stuff us
Imagine our majority once critters run for office.
While it's Bonzo this an' bonzo that an' "Bonzo, go drop dead."

But it's "Bonzo, walk in front, sir," when the camera light
  is red.
The camera light is red, my monks, the camera light is red.
It's "Bonzo, promenade now" when the camera light is red.

You talk o' lower tax for us an' bombs an' jobs an' all;
It's hard to hear that claptrap when our backs' against the wall.
An' every time you shoot yer yap the hungry folks all lose.
I'm headin' for the White House where I'm crappin' on yer shoes.
 For it's Bonzo this an' Bonzo that an'"Bonzo, groom your fleas,"
But it's "Hollywood's great monkey" on the R.K.O. marquees.
 An it's Bonzo this an' Bonzo that--I don't care what he says
For Bonzo ain't no bloody fool--He's smarter than the Pres!

LEDA AND THE SWINE

by MacBride (William Butler Yeats' guinea pig)

The snort, basso profundo: hooves come a-clopping
Up to the swooning girl, her legs hugged by pigtail
By rough porcine maleness, her hair mussed in dropping,
The oinker's lost captive has her nigh the slop pail.

Can there be resistance to forceful pig onslaught,
Or reasoned response to a lust-snorting snout?
And can there be hope for meditative thought
When so much ham's trembling and mucking about?

A gutter of the soul's encapsuled thus:
The broken fence, abandoned yard and barn
As Castor, Pollux look on.
                    They're interested
By mom and brute in wallow's nest.
Did she suspect the pig, was she forsworn
Before the porker squealed, performed and fled.

"A white cat in the desert"

by Maggie (Stephen Crane's adopted alleycat)

A white cat in the desert
Ate from a full sprig of catnip.
Suddenly was the black and crimson
Clash of dogs.
Bodies of kittens
Dotted the bright dunes.
The cat did not understand this.
He squeaked, "Why is this?"
Whereupon the dogs rushed and howled,
Gnashed and pounced
In a clamor that shook the heavens.
Still he did not understand.

PUTTY POLLY SINGS

by Legree (Paul Lawrence Dunbar's parrot)

Dis ain't no time to squawk, Pol--
 So hush now ef you can.
Fo' what's de use of singin'
 When de cou'ts acquit de Klan?
Dey's offin' folks in Greensb'ro
 Wheh racists pull de strings'
Take shots in Chatanooga
 While Putty Polly sings.

Dey's messin' wif de schools now
 An' twist folk heads real good,
Give rich folk schoolin' money
 An' rob po' kids of food.
Malindy's class is fo'ty-eight
When dat ole schoolbell rings
An' half of dem's got textbooks
 While Putty Polly sings.

Li'l Polly want a crackah
 In dat little gildy cage?
Dey's bunches in de Senate
 Who push submin'mum wage.
Dey talks like we could live on dat
 All smilin' like dey's kings
All settin' fat an' sassy
 While Putty Polly sings.

Oh Polly she's a putty boid
 Wit' feathers fine an' green
As sweet an' cute a creature
 As anybody's seen.
De rich folks never mind dat cage,
 How she never use dose wings,
All dey ever seem to want
 Is dat Putty Polly sings.

41

So ef you wants to sing now
  Sing so's we hyeahs de soun'!
Cuz Bessie Smith don't sing no mo'
  An' Billie's in de groun'.
We hyeahs so many mockin'-boids
  Chant mockins 'till it stings
An' maybe things won't be so down
  Ef Putty Polly sings.

You know, back in Sout' Africa
  Our taxes buys the aid
Dat beats up Steven Biko
  An' makes his insides bleed?
Sout' Africa it votes wit' us
  On policies an' things
We's told dat dey's our buddies
  While Putty Polly sings.

At de Civil Rights commission
  Dere expression's toinin' cold.
Dey hates affirm'tive action
  'Cuz nobody's bootstrap's pulled.
Dey hates ingrates an' welfare states
  An' enforced school busings;
But get wet in de safety net
  As Putty Polly sings.

De army eat de children.
  De lan'lor' eat de pay.
An' all of our best choices
  Are to o'ganize an' pray.
Hey--kin you sing a anthem?
  While we ain't all Doctah Kings
Dere ain't no way to stay dis way.
  Sing, Putty Polly, sing!

TO AN OSTRICH DYING YOUNG

by Shropshire Chick (A.E. Housman's flamingo)

The time you ran from lion the race
Was yours--no contest in that chase.
We cheered you on, loud and full-hearted;
I laughed until my rib-cage smarted.

To-day, the path where Big Bird wobbles
We plod, not racing down the cobbles
And set you in your sandy bed
Where you used to stick your head.

Fat bird, you leave as summer goes
On crazy legs and doubled toes.
As thistles spring from shifting sand
They tumble off to no-man's land.

Eyes shut by the desert night
Can't see by the dawn's early light,
Cacophany and lone songs sung
Are all alike in earth's dull tongue.

No more will you gallop through
The marketplace, leave booths askew,
Or haul ass over ridge and hill,
Bird ever flightless, ever still.

We set, as you go toward your rest,
Your egg in fame's eternal nest,
And set, for future outsized fowl
Your legacy beside the Owl.

And 'round that youthful, pin-sized head
Will flock to gaze the birdie dead
And find on you nor tears nor sorrow
But feathers lighter than a sparrow.

THIRTEEN WAYS OF LOOKING AT A HERRING

by Chameleon as in the Letter C
(Wallace Stevens' broad-ranging lizard)

I

I watched for silence
in the ocean.
Beside me there was silence.
Before me
fish broke their backs
against the rocks.
Awaiting me
was a single herring.

II

Sharks will not eat herring
because it is so hard
to prepare one properly.

III

I looked up lost
like a herring
in an ocean of ink
like a herring
in a thought balloon.

IV

A man and a woman
are one.
A man and a woman and a herring
are three.

V

Along the shore
the sky opens

to smells that free the air.
The flaming clatter
of a beautiful woman's comb,
the clear whistle
of a fresh herring.

VI

The morning chatters.
The herrings are having tea.

VII

The sun left us
without a whisper
as the imagined heart of a herring.

VIII

He owned a baseball team
and half the newspapers in the state.
Rich men
bid for his kleenex.
He had the brain of a herring.

IX

The herring interrupts nothing.
He swims
in a boat of light.

X

Over half a million
tons of sardines
are harvested annually
from the Pacific Ocean.
It never storms at sea.
It is only the sky wailing
for the herring without eyelids.

XI

The earth turns to darkness
like a herring in the fall.

XII

When the ocean freezes
the crafty herrings
swim warm
in the blood of our memories.

XIII

For the price of a Veg-O-Matic
you could not buy
the stealth of a herring.

POULTRY

by Edsel (Marianne Moore's retriever)

When well-fed, they're disgusting: significant as bloodbloated
fleas.
  Hungry, however, one can find even in a chicken, the soul
  of a peahen, the savor of a turkey.
    Claws that can scratch, eyes
    milky from imbecility, feathers matted
      from filth and vermin, but this stuff isn't important

When one considers that a chicken is only partly meal and partly
  a function to be interpreted. Yes, a function--we all
  need chickens as we need food:
    the canine cannot question good
    or evil when his stomach growls
      or try to extract hegemony from the distant howls

of wolves or other dogs because as we have noted, the basic
  law we are observing is chicken. An imaginative
  dog can see a chicken as the drive
    shaft in the engine life;
    the well-oiled gear
      which slick as rain

powers the locomotive bringing in the car of Gravy Train;
  we must, however, differentiate
  chicken from soymeal and polybenzoate.
    This we don't need
    at time of feed.
      Better to be genuine, jump the high

fence to the chicken yard, go for real blood and white meat.
  There is no substitute for organic fowl, and among us no dogs
  can afford to be
    "liberalists of
    their machinations"--above
      convenience and slimy timidity there's nutrition

to think of and "imaginary garbage with real mould in it" is all
Ralston-Purina would feed us, given the chance. Hear:
the rich warmth of a fresh
  killed rooster amid winter snow
  is all ye know of poultry and civilization
    and all ye need to know.

TWEETY AMONG THE NIGHTENGALES

by Old Possum (T.S. Eliot's cat)

ὤμοι, πέπληγμαι καιρίαν πληγὴν ἔσω.

Noneck Tweety jumps on swing
Jiggling little birdie fat,
The sentence springs from orange jaw,
"I tought I taw a putty-tat."

In darkness of the cartoon night
Figures move on painted stage,
Death and Sylvester skulking near
As Tweety sings in gilded cage.

On stepladder the cat climbs high,
Precarious in darkened room.
Door opens, rug slides, and the poor
Putty-tat fall down. Go boom.

Gloomy Elmer and the Hare
In the moonlit garden stalk;
Elmer hunts the rabbit's lair
And Bugsy says, "Eh--what's up, doc?"

A desert bird roars through the scene
Sprawling objects everywhere;
In shadowed corner, a wiley
Coyote runs claws through his hair.

This clever vertebrate will draw
A deadly Acme Avis Bomb,
Slip up when he's about to throw
And blow himself to hell and gone.

These desert fauna are long gone.
Sylvester's over his surprise,
Decides a new gambit to try
With sharpened claws and glassy eyes.

49

He leaves the room to head outside,
Up the trellis rails he scamps,
Out of the wisteria
Through the window, long he jumps

And golden. Down comes cage and stand;
Rage's claws tear cage doors clear.
The nightengales are singing near
Where Putty-tat scarfs Tweety-dear

And sang all through that bloody night
As Daffy cried with mourning blokes,
Their liquid tears were Tweety's shroud
And thi-thi-thi-thi-thi-that's all, folks.

THE NEW GALOSHES

by Fabian (Emma Lazarus' terrier)

Unable to turn the knob with Greek design,
With trembling limbs, I cry out my remand;
Inside our rain-drenched, puddled porch I stand--
An anxious dog needing a walk, whose whine
Is all nature imprisoned. This title's mine:
"Mother of Impatience." Beside umbrella, and boots prone
The new galoshes lie, dry as a bone.
The storm makes windows chant in lightning's shine.
"Keep, timid ones, your tootsies dry!" says me
With growling throat. "Give me your open door.
Your huddled mastiff's yearning for a tree
Before my refuse steams on your bright floor
Send me, your lawnless, temper-strained out free!"
I lift my leg beside the cuspidor.

THE GIFT UPRIGHT

by Monktime (Robert Frost's chimpanzee)

The man was ours before we were the man.
He was Homo Erectus more than an aeon
Before we walked like people. Our mirror
In Peking, across the Bering,
But we were Darwin's, still simians
Peeling bananas while they just slid by,
Peeling while they called us unappealing.
The branches we held made us weak in the legs
Until we found it was our defeat
But willing to walk from the wood of surrender
We reached for the skies while grasped firm with our toes.
Weak as we were, we brought ourselves upright
(The act of standing was an act of grace)
To the sight of the socialized monkey-man
We donned our Nehru jackets and manbags
As human as you and as cool as we can.

MY PUPPY'S WALTZ

by The Lost Mutt (Theodore Roethke's boxer)

Fermented doggie breath
Very nearly overtook us;
We'd eaten what was left
Of the rum cake and dope cookies.

We romped until our shanks
Were sore as hell from romping,
While over in the flanks
Ted set to do some stomping.

The hand whose anger struck
Was righteous, sure, and sound;
He said that for a buck
He'd fetch us to the pound.

Our yips sunk in the rugs,
Then silence drunk the noise.
We slept that night like dogs
And dreamed of damp rag toys.

any pup lived in a pretty cow town

by & etc (E.E. Cummings' dog)

any pup lived in a pretty cow town
(with how so happy doggies there does)
mutt schnauzer sheepdog pointer
he woofed his wasn't he waved his was

cowgirls and cowboys (both short and fat)
tossed anypup curses   kick and rattle
they branded their bubbles they dogged their cat
spur cinch bridle saddle

youngsters thought (for just a while
for puberty popped and parts appeared)
that they would make their anypup smile
bone ball whisper tear

here by where and girl by boy
she wet his papers she chewed his toy
starling by window and wood by stove
anypup's any was puppies for love

underdog mated with overdog
whimpered their stickings and hopped their hope
(growl waggle leg and beg)
ate their evers and fertiled their egg

bush pole hydrant tree
(and only the dogs can make them see)
and puppies don't know of their cap or their crown
with up so ugly and many goose down

one day doggie heaven was beckoning sweet
(and nobody missed him down under his feet)
anydogs joined the perpetual puzzle
wiggle by waggle and muzzle by muzzle

if by any and dreams by drugs
and mutt by mutt they sleep like dogs
nomutt by anymutt season by spring
romp by rainbow and song by sing

cowgirls and cowboys (moonlight and guitar)
cinch saddle bridle spur
get along little doggies and yipee-yi-yi
cloud airplane wind sky

THE HORSE THAT THROUGH THE GREEN HUES DRIVES THE HOUF

by Milkwood (Dylan Thomas' Shetland pony)

The horse that through the green hues drives the hours
Drives my racing speed; that kicks the clods of sod
Is my last pasture.
And I may never address the rosey winner's wreath
As hoof-and-mouth scratches the edges of my breath.

The horse that drives the milk cart through the alleys
Drives my long sinew, lanking down familiar trails
To where bare-bone lies.
And I, once known as "Handsome Hide," my frayed and stringy tail
Will slow and gandy swing, a nest for horseflies.

The hoof that pounds alfalfa in the trough
Pounds the glue; that heaves the ropes of plows
Heaves my belly off.
And I tie the knots of my sweeneyd shoulder to ash
As ash dampened is clay, so is muscle to earth.

The hackney draws love's cart to the corral
Where hayseed glints in sun, a jewel
For sore eyes.
And I will canter high in spiced wind
As time with even hand bridles us all.

And I will trot where burros sway and plod
Across night's blind and endless paths of sod.

THE GRIZZLY SKUNK

by Fifi (Galway Kinnell's polecat)

1

Two weeks from Wednesday
in a dream, I think
I will root
magpies
from the light in the forest.
I will bend
the leaves from the grass
and spiders will be there
bleeding,
splayed,
another, another
and when it is finished
it will be the broken and blubbery
ghost of an angel.

2

Clattering,
a grizzly skunk
roots into cabbage rot
and disappears.

3

I loll across the swollen meadows.
If I were a person
I would be
the skydiver
falling the long parabola of skunk angst
falling into dumpster
of fragmented Pepsi bottles.

There I will lie,
still and broken,
a bit smelly to the others
licking
the sticky insemination of soot with which I write.

THE YOGHURT FILLING FUJI

by Monkey (Gary Snyder's monkey)

Naked boys from Petaluma
sing prayers
while climbing from the mountain.
    All day they have been
    sweating and praying,
harvesting the locusts.   A horse

    in the field
is reflected--surely from
    the eye
        of the Buddha.
What of it?
    The boys know
        but won't tell us.
They grin mystically in
    their small circle.
        The Buddha's light
gleams on their bare butts.   They grunt.
The horse grunts.
    It is raining green tea on the flatlands.

LASSIE

by Crow (Sylvia Plath's black Labrador)

You are not her, you are not her
Any more, mangy cur.
You're not the silvery queen of the screen
Any more than I am Rin-Tin-Tin.
It's all make-up, your robelike fur.

Lassie, in my mind, I bit you.
Your star was fading
When I was a pup;
How do you measure a puppy up
To a holy Collie of virgin birth?

Though in your head, you only know
You command a higher wage than Garbo
You've a brutish head,
No thoroughbred.
You've commanded me like a German Shepherd.

Your happy barks of rescue
Supplication and yes, speech
Sounded more like nothing each
Time than martial orders.
Achtung.

It grabbed me like a steel trap.
I felt it in my paws.
Whenever you saved the family fair
I felt the lie, I gasped for air;
Yip, yip, yip, yip, yip--

Lassie, when I was a puppy
I had the S.P.C.A. put you to sleep.
With your long handsome stride
I felt pudgy inside
like a lumpy dummkopf dachshund.

No dog of love, I see you
Tearing after a fleeing Jew
From the death camp,
Or set on a freedom rider
By some southern cop

And always aiming for the jugular.
Always straining at the leash
And growling, howling
Your every thought of disembowelling.
A collar of twin lightning bolts, you--
Not *bow-wow* but really *sig heil*.
Not a communication in the barks
But a Liederkranz of threats
Your image so strong I'd often get
Like a cat

All pissy and fur on end.
Your mane, your mane
Blond as the perfect race is blond.
I was two when you left the screen.
That's fourteen in people years.

I lit out for Hollywood myself
To get to you, maybe share a bone,
Then they threw me in the cellar all alone
When they caught me.
So Lassie, I bury the bone now.

The doggie chews are out with the trash.
The squeaker toy is burned to ash.
The sock they'd throw
Is beneath yellow snow
To a place we could both never dig.

Though beefsteak's in your little fat gut
The producers did not respect you.
They were just cashing in on you.
From the banks all your lifeblood they drew.
Lassie, Lassie, you bitch, I'm through.

from GROWL

by Solomon (Allen Ginsberg's husky)

I saw the best mutts of my germination destroyed by badness, stuffed
   rhinestoned jacketed,
leashed along through the burbs at dawn looking for an empty lawn,
mongrelheaded fangsters searching Ursa Major for the dominoe'd
   dalmation bond of earth and sky,
who'd wept in poverty on floors of musicians and wept in marijuana
   cloud of backlit dumps at city roof contemplating meat,
who bared their teeth to mailmen from under the Porch and saw wild
   Arabian dog packs glow skyward,
who passed through playgrounds with sleepy red eyes hallucinating
   Dogpatch and Rin-Tin-Tin heroics among the Canine Corps,
who were booted from obedience school for mad dog and messing
   obscene piles on windowsills,
who trembled in doghouses in winter, burning their toys in ashen ground
   listening to whistles of wind through broken board,
who got busted by dogcatchers returning home after toppling garbage cans
   at the Ritz,
who sickened from meat undercooked in Paradise's own goulash,
   untempered by mercy,
incomparable back alleys of life and dead rodent, and lightning
   damp run to the sunbeams at street end,
who leashed themselves to lamp posts before the endless pedestrian
   traffic of Brooklyn night life, with Monkee boots and miniskirts
   and sandaled holy men benzedrined mouthwracked mumbling the
   eternal in walking river past the ancient curbside shore,
who holed at night in blinking neon of Eastside Ristorantes of
   the hunger of neglectedness, while cables sparked staccato
   electric harmony on the rooftops,
who bit open helium balloons with the intellectual teeth and breathed
   deeply to do Muppet impersonations in Rimbaud's mammal warm night,
Coyote solidarities of hunt and moon prayer over wide open field
   of needle-pocked sky, darkness vibrations in cold desert of city
   freeze and mind of radio noise in clear air,
who cornered longhaired Jewish or Hindu animals at synagogue steps
   claiming they were on a rabbi hunt of chanting Hare Krishna,
who panted down the August beach at Coney Island semiconscious from
   summer's dog days, weaving and maniacal hot dogs,
who dug the sweet bop earth of a million back yards across Kansas

and Idaho to hide the beefsteak bones of newly departed steer
  souls to the strident ahimsa of midwest dinner tables,
who prowled the subway entrances of Rochester on paws and knees
  to be kicked out by faceless businessmen with teeth missing
  from their faces that weren't there,
who bit cats on the tail and laughed hysterically at the clawmarks on
  their noses laughing at their own silly blood and the ladies who
  pointed and shouted while wearing dead animals,
who gathered at the stage door of the opera singing Verdi choruses
  wild and freeform to sweeten the perfumed onyx pomp of fat culture
  and nightmare,
who coughed in sickness and dedication outside a Kansas City club
  where Bird made the call of all flesh rise supreme to the hip
  cacophony of universal pleasure/pain anarchy,
who howled out car windows in parking lots of shopping malls, the
  displays of mass market and Christmas lights and hedonistic
  Capitalist product crashing like shards of planets through their
  eyes,
who created great spectacles of fang and jowl atop amphitheater park
  stages remaking Midsummer Bite's Dream and Chihuahua at Colonus,
who ran to the forests of Canadian wildlife unknown barking French
  oaths of runic dogeating ceremonies,
returning weeks later visible maddog ragged coat full of thistle
  and hallucinogenic beat syntax refusing to be bathed and singing
  elemental dirges, if you don't know how to do it, I'll show
  you how to walk the dog,
Ah Allen while you are not me and I am not you, and now you're really
  in the duck soup of word celebrity,
and therefore we can see that these are illusions, too, when you
  write that a man's best friend is his best friend's genitalia
  or I sculpt twentieth century skeltonics on schnauzer ass--
Recreate with me the golden diorama of godhead's watchdog sixheaded
  playing musical fanfare for the suffering of America's domestic
  prisoner of species imperialism
with the absolute heat of ovulation torn from an eternity of litter
  borning anew.

TRYING TO TALK WITH A CAT

by Lucretia Mott (Adrienne Rich's goldfinch)

Out in this forest we're of the safari.

What else could bring us here?

Sometimes I feel like the free wind
surging up through canyons
angling erosion process
by its own choice and sculpture
into this threatening grove.

On agreement, we made this real challenge--
leaving behind the sappy idylls like Tom & Jerry,
the ancient prophecies of the cat laying down with the bird,
the game of catch-and-escape we were
featured in our first spring days, the competition
for crumbs, the warm-day detente
hours of restfulness
ignoring each other--

Perched here
on this branch, I look into the fierce, flashing
face of cat below making dull
clucking, hunting noise
like a skeleton rattling
a haunted house
of the head

It sounds like the nerves of this scene
but we brought it here
as everyday
As blood/heart thump in our ears
coming here was our shackle

In fluff I feel more fragile
near you than away
As you sharpen fang and claw
on bark

we talk of cooperation in mutual
adversity--I notice
your hunger grow

Your powerful uniform of appetite--
--The Salivation Army--
Your epaulettes of birdie claw
jostling as you begin your circle
We talk of agreement
as if we were birdbrains
as if we were lovebirds in Paris.

TAILS

by Popa (Charles Simic's cat)

My den is lined with rat tails.
I prize my trophies, I display them
Proudly to my friends,
And as warnings to my enemies
In the night streets.

Sometimes when half drowsing
I think I hear them
Tapping like little soft drums on the walls,
Soft as an imbecile hears the rain
On the butcher's slanted roof.

My inner body cleans its claws.
No rats brings me rest
Like blood makes the heart rejoice
Like the logger inside the tree
Makes the tree strong
On newly leased federal land.

INDEX OF POETS

Other Books by David Shevin

Expecting Ginger Rogers (1975)
Camptown Spaces (1978)
Postcard: Bebe 1909 (1978)
The Stop Book (1978)
What Happens (1983)
The Discovery of Fire (1988)

ABOUT THE EDITOR: David Shevin received his pedigrees at Bowling Green State University (M.F.A.) and the University of Cincinnati (Ph.D.), and is Assistant Professor of English at Tiffin University. His collections of poetry include *What Happens* (1983) and *The Discovery of Fire* (1988). He serves with the Executive Committee of the U.S. Peace Council and the New Jewish Agenda Task Force on Central America.

ABOUT THE EDITOR'S CAT: Tuna Shevin, a leading deconstructionist critic of contemporary furniture, lectures in Kitty Litterature at Catatonic State. In the radical 1960's, she translated the American edition of *Quotations from Chairman Miaow* and collaborated with Tabby Hoffman on *Scratch This Book.* As Chair of Pussycats for Social Responsibility, she currently puts most of her efforts into the "Star Wars Gives Me Hairballs" campaign.

PRAISE FOR

The Discovery of Fire

by David Shevin

Winner of the 1989 Ohioana Book Award for Poetry

Shevin has such "a naturally wide range of subject, that he accomplishes that very difficult feat of bringing the personal together with the political, as they should be."

--Bruce Weigl

"David Shevin...is an 'engaged' rather than confessional or private poet. His poems speak to every aspect of being human, the public concerns that bind us in a community as well as the private concerns where we recognize our personal dignity. Although the reader can easily guess where Shevin's political sympathies lie, his poems are never dogmatic of ideological."

--Robert Fox, *Airfare*

"*The Discovery of Fire* is a literate, political gem, a work of satirical savagery reminiscent of a cross between Brecht at his nastiest and Neruda at his least 'artistic.' ...We need David Shevin, a truly *artistic* topical poet, and a *savagely* good moralist."

--*People's Culture*

Available from Bottom Dog Press, c/o Firelands College, Huron, Ohio 44839